Through Broken Windows

Katie Rigdon

Presentation by *BookLeaf Publishing*

Web: www.bookleafpub.com

E-mail: info@bookleafpub.com

ISBN: 9789357440097

First edition 2023

To my loving and enduring husband Kenny. You have made my dreams of love and life come true and you are truly a rock in my life.

ACKNOWLEDGEMENT

I cannot express enough that even though my road in life has been painful, unstable and filled with guilt and uncertainty, I have never lost sight of our creator, Jehovah, and his undeserved kindness. I would not be here today if it were not for him and his word the Bible which has always brought me back to faith and the belief there was a future for me with purpose.

PREFACE

This is my season. This is my winter. A time of ending things, of putting things to rest. The season of rotting and death that gives way to a clean canvas; Snowy white! A canvas that longs for rebirth, and in it I shall start my journey to find my purpose in life.

An Honest Reflection

When the mirror is a liar, our souls rest easy. For we do not see our own selves, we see only our desired estimate.

Secretly we judge the truth of our character, finding the hollows, and as we meet those who bare distasteful qualities and imperfections so similar to our own, we measure them, and we condemn them.

While loathing them is unwarranted and shameful, we find it brings us a balance. For we dare not scorn at our own reflection. So we wage war on the parts of us we hate, by despising the mirror that tells the truth.

Alice

She cannot see it, how could she be it, still, the image she despised in the mirror has come into focus.

It's so clear now, she knows what she must do, but inside she battles the bruises so black and blue is the color of her heart.

Pale dewy face and tight pursed lips, fidgeting white fingertips. Cd cases with residue, and one dollar bills she snorts her life through.

Is it freedom she seeks or pain she avoids, how many shovels of powder to fill the void?

What corners will she turn while she destroys, every last fucking hope of a normal life, all to satisfy the ferocious devil known as Snow White.

Just one she says, one line is a joke. Just one she says, only one gram of coke.
50 gone a hundred spent, after midnight her money's spent. Death dealers on speed dial, posting up in her head, they pay no rent, they pay no mind, speed dial and a few more miles she drives back to her prison, an axe to grind.

Her enemy is not the razor or the chunk of sweet ether magic. Her burden is bound for tragedy and traffic, her inner voice screams

FANATIC! FANATIC! But that's nonsense. Go, go, go down the rabbit hole. But if only Alice knew how big her habit grew.

A mountain of a girl washed away by an avalanche, trees, rocks, plants, and love she grasps for. But she reaches out and there's nothing to cling to, not even a foothold. So out she goes to find her fix; what will be next? Her deeds unforetold. Except for the burden of that unfillable hole.

She's searching, she's tripping, eyes rolled back she's dipping in and out of her sub-conscience. It's nonsense. Faking, breaking, shattered, mistaken thinking that one fuck will make her that girl, will make her desirable.

She's misunderstood as a lap girl, a fast girl, a tap it just once girl, and she's so much more.

I'm Not Okay

I'm tired of looking at my face, bleach in the closet, dust on the bookcase. I stare out the window, but all I see is the window, took out the trash threw out my dildos. I'm even tired of fucking myself these days. My stomach aches from munching on boredom and pity, but I'm trying to digest it, it doesn't matter though my cabinets are full of it there's just a steady flow of shit nothing good on TV except the Canadian fucking Parliament, and man, I don't speak French.

How much time does it take to count the hairs on my forearm, I should be done before my alarm goes off in the morning, God, boring ain't the word for it.

Quick, pick me out a new life before I end the present slice of pie my ass, bowl of cherries, why are we comparing our journey to fruit? Fruitless Katie, react more. Get up walk out the door look for my ride, no car in sight, just another reminder of the approaching night. With the dark comes blushed cheeks, flushed cheeks from frustration, I'm caged in! Where's the Tempo of my salvation?

Am I imploding or exploding I don't know?
I'm just a mess from head to toe, longing for the
storm of yesterday, God's show; Clouds flying
by, wind throwing things into unnatural places I
pleaded my case with the sky. But I'm still here,
the wind didn't move, 140 lbs of "God why did
you do this to me". I wanted the fame now
who's to blame for my own success? Try
this...Fuck less.

I feel the itch of my evil side. She's critical and
sneering, slightly domineering, she brags: "I can
fix this while you drag your sorry ass out of my
way". "Okay, okay so it's been a month and I
haven't fixed it", I spit. "But I want to try this
way called right. Something you'd know nothing
about, miss quick-to-open-your-mouth, you
don't fight shit".

So, what if my battle is invisible. It's divisible,
head, heart, body and soul, casualties taking
their toll. My bleeding trail is all that bewails
me.

No call, no show. I've got no phone to expect
to ring, no friends collecting me, so I call
collect. A pass by in a day or two if they can, "I
just can't believe this is happening to you man"
is the consolation I get. A fit of rage wells up
inside, all I want is a fucking ride and a
cigarette! I don't care where we go just help me
forget I'm losing everything I have.

Back to the kitchen and open the pot of leftovers is all I got of the being I once was. I hear the voices from my evil side whisper "it's just us can we come in?" No man, it's my kitchen! I can't have peace anywhere! It's bad enough you're camped between my ears, and you operate my fears. I won't let you scare me though. The bottle of Tylenol poses more of a threat than the old me, Evil Katie, just don't pity yourself.

I haven't starved yet, so I don't worry I just bury my pen in my book to let out the pain and what it took from me. But I'm not taken as far as giving up. I'll strut my sorry butt to bed first, imagining good night kisses. The wishes I pray for comfort me....and sleep will come eventually.

A Poem For Patrick

There are so many words I fumbled over yesterday, trying to tell you what I wanted to say. The sentences came out incomplete, and I wish that while they
still hung in the air, I could have rearranged them in a sensible way.

Trying to bend a thought to sound the way it is felt, is harder than I imagined when staring into your eyes. How can I explain what I never let myself acknowledge? How do I put into words the emotions under disguise?

Lust and companionship sounded better than nothing, and without regret I look back on whatever we had in those moments. But when faced with goodbye the lust is not consolation enough. I wanted the passion, to scream it, to own it.

I do not feel cheated because this affair was one-sided, but I cherish the affection you never neglected to give. Sometimes it felt like it meant more than attraction, but I climbed down from that cloud, it was more comfortable for me to suppress it, than let that dream live.

I want you to know how proud I am of you for taking control of your life and moving on, but it stings to know that we're already drifting apart. I never had any expectations of you Patrick, but no matter what I tried to stop it from happening, you still managed to occupy a special place in my heart.

I hope when you think about me somewhere far away, I will make you laugh at something I did or said. If you do, it is only because you made it so easy for me to be myself around you. In your company, my insecurities laid still in my head.

A part of me is angry with you because of your indifference; I know our quiet moments will soon be nothing more than a distant thought. But after you leave, I'm sure I will force myself to forget before long, only in the web of my dreams will our memories be caught.

I hope you don't think I'm silly or stupid for writing this poem, but actually I take that back, because on paper I can organize what I wanted yesterday for you to hear. Now that the fog of my drinking has been lifted, I can express what, before, was hidden by fear.

Thank you for all the fun we had together but fuck you for what we didn't evolve to. You made me realize what I have to offer someone, someday; I'm not heartbroken to know it won't involve you.

Drive safe and have good times while you are still young, seize the moment, love hard, and learn more. May God watch over you for all of your days, and good luck in the world's you explore.

I hope today when I see you, I will have the courage to ask you, to kiss me like you will never be able to kiss me again. Maybe in that moment with our bodies pressed together you will love me, for that moment, and I will finally let go of my friend.

But This Woman Is Not Me

Somewhere there is a woman; she is holding a baby girl tight. She loves to gaze upon her, all throughout the night. She has fallen hard for her baby number three........ But this woman is not me.

Somewhere there is a woman; she has worked a long and tiring day. She goes home knowing the difference she made to all. She thinks her day a success as she sips her tea.............. But this woman is not me.

Somewhere there is a woman, who has won the admiration of her son's teachers with her dedication to helping to further the classes' education. She is favored by all the young ones she sees....... But this woman is not me.

Somewhere there is a woman; she is looking into her husband's eyes. She's so in love still, she has given him a surprise for their five-year anniversary....... But this woman is not me.

Somewhere there is a woman; she has taken her mother on a cruise. They sit and enjoy the sun and drink a little booze. They rejoice over their wonderful day floating atop the wavy sea....... But this woman is not me.

Somewhere there is a woman; she has a brother-in-law as a friend. They laugh and talk as they BBQ; the whole family is at ease...... But this woman is not me.

Somewhere there is a woman, she is letting down her hair. It flows past her shoulders and down to her waist, she combs it softly........ But this woman is not me.

Somewhere there is a woman, she is cooking in her home. She has planned a special dinner for the reunion of her family........ But this woman is not me.

Somewhere there is a woman; she is straightening her cap and gown. She's so excited, she's worked so hard, she goes up to the stage to except her degree....... But this woman is not me.

Somewhere there is a woman, she is talented and smart. She has overcome her boundaries and written a book of poetry......... But this woman is not me.

Somewhere there is a woman; she is strong and exemplary in her faith. She has chosen a road many cannot take; she's left home to be a missionary........ But this woman is not me.

Somewhere there is a woman; she would never cry herself to sleep........ But this woman is not me.

Mom

I take a look around at what's left to pack. Shifting hopes and dreams back and forth, out the door goes my life literally. Pitifully I accept the truth of what I just couldn't do.

Facing forward peering into the future, ya gotta love living with mother, the time spent there will be the suture that never heals the wound. Looking back, it was the tomb of my serenity. To infinity and beyond, reaches the pessimistic attitude of my mom offers nothing but a roof over my head.

I love and hate that she forgives, only to berate, our relationship is the unhealthiest I've ever had. More than all my ex's and toss in my dad and it's a close call. My head falls at the thought of future battles. Tests, without the keys, without a book to study. Please tell me it's worth the rattle of my soul. A woman out of control without the knowledge of the toll it takes on I, it takes on my ever-shrinking self-image.

The line of scrimmage has been crossed; this game is best lost by both teams. Two women who see their beauty, no more feuding is my biggest dream.

How do we dissolve the pain and the reign of our demons? How do we resolve to change the beings we've depended on to protect us? The evil Bitches we became left us molded and pressed us into the mom's we detested.

 "If you only saw things my way" I might as well say. My stubbornness came from her, and it's impossible to deter this woman from her road of misery, impossible for her to add up history. Multiply "I'll never forgive you" times "I'll never let the injury leave my mind" equals pain longer, a strain stronger than love in our home.

 Our hearts are where it all starts, and I can't change hers, but mine is debatable, the routine that I've carted around with me for so long, hate-able. But if I let go God, please can you, send me my "How not to kill your mother manual"?

 Anticipating hurtful words with good intentions, brings anticipated words with good intentions, might I mention frustration, a generous pension of sorts, has caused me to resort to tears, "I hate You's" and my fears of doing more damage than good usually rings true.

 I go for a drive to scream out the madness of it all. "Why me, why me?" is the call I manage. I slap on a half-assed bandage to stop the sting, but the pain still stays true, the blood still bleeds

through, no more mom kissing boo-boos
goodbye is what I've said a million times to my
childhood memories, Mom I
miss you.

I can't sort out where to lay the blame, I'm
tired of playing the game of who deserves to
inflict the pain, because I smell foul on every
other play. Every other day there is a reason to
call a penalty.

I long for the tenderly said "I love You's, made
up mom and daughter rituals, the habitual
actions of healthy families.

I can't stand to be neurotic. No sugar coated "I
got it's" because I don't. I won't ever recover if I
keep walking backwards into the storm saying
it's normal to conform to this approach.

With eyes on the prize, I can focus on my half
of the problem, breath in and keep calm and
change my perspective of the mom I've grown
to know so well, the mom I've told to go to hell
a hundred times now I owe a hundred apologies.

What's wrong with me? Who am I to use
psychology against someone else?
Bless Mom, change Me.

Die Slow

Guilt and pain are the perfect motivation, but first you have to sin. Go ahead, and like the others let the devil in and swim in the failures that will turn you to the broad path. The aftermath is never what you wanted, the rewards go unrewarded, and you wallow in your pity for lack of a better response.

It's such a complicated mess, it's so dull and fucking relentless how I live on, and yet I can't live at all. Falling in love is not permitted and guards are set to keep you committed to the course. No detouring, no skipping a beat, you must finish what you started and deal with the echo of your footsteps on empty streets. Because no one walks your path but you.

Insomnia and booze keep you company instead of your knight in shining armor, and the harbor of your heart has pined for one sailor to dock, just one to come ashore. All I ever wanted was one more. Why must I wait here and rot away inside, day after day, dying from the genocide of love lacking?

Whitewashed but bearing a scarlet letter, I try to look up to God and not feel cheated and shamed all at the same time. You have the power to make it better. Time is never on my side. So, I say fuck trying because I'm tired and lying feels like truth unbridled.

Am I wrong to question everything? Isn't that what we are supposed to do? Look, and search, and die to find the answers that will bring us closer to you?

Blue days, and red nights paint the pages of the book of my life. A wife is all I ever wanted to be. Twist the knife one more time what difference does it make now, my vows to you I've never lived up to. I've always had the why, but never the how. Just let me go…. let me die slow.

There Was Two

Cameron... Where are you now when I need you? I don't know how to feel through this maze help me awake from my daze. How many days has it been since I've seen you. You only pop in now and then since the day of my decision, it was the right one, but I still miss the fun we had sometimes two minds seemed better than one. So how come we always got into so much trouble together? Two birds of a feather, two peas in a pod, Siamese if you please but we never plotted for a good cause.

I always let you take the lead run the show be the star, you always had me on my knees be the hoe bare the scar, now I'm trying not to bleed from this hole in my heart but I'm starting to believe our souls are better off apart.

I let you call it as you see it, I'd hand over the reins you'd pick up the pain and seize it squeeze it caress it and tease it. Like Don Juan to sex, your skills came so correct but it's just when I've said I'm never left home alone you evacuate it.

Shit, you deceived me with this false sense of security like a rent-a-cop with an inclination to be dirty. I should have seen the signs of your crimes they were so obvious to a layman, now I'm left blaming myself for not escaping the wealth of your shaming.

You had to be dancing in the bars, getting drunk, make the dough; you had me climbing out of cars getting fucked smoking dro's. Now I'm trying to depart from the trunk switching roles, Ya see I've gotten kind of smart while looking up from the floor.

My head is pounding with confusion, as I begin to heal from your bruising. If to feel is to heal and to heal is to feel, I hold strong to the real fuck your comfortable appeal.

I hire help to sort through your lies, file after file without compromise I measure the depth of my demise, the girth of my shame, the length of the pain. Fuck name calling, words can't contain what I've been through thanks to you on page 582 of a journal without capacity to hold even a few of the life experiences that need to be told.

What have you done for me lately, oh yeah that's right, you got me high as a kite. Now don't get me wrong the sky's a nice place to visit, but I could still hear the ants below bitching that I'm blocking all the sunlight.
Damn.......do you remember it the same way I do?

I mostly recall you asking for my assistance
Katie. You were afraid to confront anything
pretending to be innocent. You were the brains
in the operation I was just your hands when you
got tired of yourself, I always had to find you a
man to lose yourself in, abuse yourself with.

The contusions on the mind we share you'll
find were there since the day you began banging
your head against the wall, multiply the pain by
two when I heard you screaming it was all my
fault.

Now while you're digging tunnels to hide in,
I'm cleaning out my nails, and even though the
boats still sinking I haven't given up on pails,
and not knowing a cork is all we need to save us
is better than just bailing, girl with a little
cooperation I can foresee smooth sailing.

I'm so sorry you saw penis as an answer to
your problem, Vic's, cocaine and a bottle for you
to crawl in. The lengths I had to go to provide a
cynical line for you to fall in, I had your back all
this time, but you never answered your calling.

This playground that we share should have
long ago been deserted; step outside the fence
Katie, the whole worlds not perverted. I know
you do not understand right now, your mind has
not yet converted but the possibilities are
endless, come on trust me. You have got to move
on in life if you want to preserve it.

Another thing you should know is I have never left I'm always within you, two souls put apart now grow closer by the same fucking issues, a child frozen in time moves forth life continued. Flowers placed on the grave of Feuds and Forgive You's. Oil and water do not mix, hope floats, count your blessings, while the wound still stings learn from your lessons, and never forget a life of purpose has a powerful message.

Where Did My Pen Go To

Say it.... just say it. I'm trying to say it, but it's not coming out the way I'd like. I can't feel the handles of the bike I'm riding through the neighborhood of this section of my life. When did my pen get so heavy I couldn't even type?

Why do I find it surprising I'm not allowed to sit and gripe about the

fact that the only way to express myself just doesn't get the words out right?

That's crap. In fact, it's a humongous pile of complicated mixed-up emotions and stories better known as a rap. Not the kind the stars do, but the kind that you fall into, wipe off of your shoes, and try not to carry around with you.

When a feeling gets lost on the way out of my head and takes a detour south, I would normally expect it to find the route most commonly taken to my mouth. But when it's on its way to the hand of a heavily medicated soul, words become too thick to swim through, and they can't afford the toll to my fingertips.

I must come to grips with my defects of character and try to make them look as shiny as rusted, busted, and tarnished can look. I took too long standing in the rain trying to wait out the storm; I've lost the form of expression I desire to use to form your mind around the sound of abnormal.

It's a swarm though, the locusts eat everything you see on the outside and then come back for the crumbs, leaving the ground of my planet lacking in emotional funds. Bankrupt is just the beginning of my problems. Just walking becomes hobbling on the sidewalk in front of any place of spiritual wealth, I need to get a daily checkup and a dose of spirituality.

My health is only as good as the questions I don't ask Dr. South; she just sticks the tongue depressor deep into my mouth and tells me to say "aaaahhhh".
Give me one more prescription Doc to add to the Sunday through
Saturday pill dispenser sitting on my desk. I got this mess inside me called bi-polar-OCD-addict what? And I tic tock like a bomb set to go off. But...... that's just what's wrong with my mind. Which kind of meds do I take for this, at which time?

Listen careful I'll tell you what else my temple can't do. I'm stuck in the body of someone 28 plus 42. Years, years go by and I'm still not happy. I do not think it is even possible to feel this crappy for such an indefinite period of time. Fast forward to the front of the line, I wonder

will I have a man to hold my hand as we exit
life, what a crime it would be really if I didn't.

It kind of feels like something was stolen from
me at some point, can I have my chance back?
My childhood persona was attacked before I had
a chance to glance back at my innocence. Give
me a break I was only coloring the clouds black
for spite.

Nathan's Song

This pain is so bad I can't envision the end of it, afraid of who I'll be without relief, afraid of my sinfulness. Suicidal thoughts creeping in, but I damper the worst of it. Shits heavy but I keep jumping to avoid the lows, avoid the blows, avoid the blow... I am scared of my own self-defenses.... Like when my anger flows. My Evil twin knocking on my windows and doors. Hate coursing through my veins. Wishing the pain would stop and my only options are homicidal, or suicidal a product of a sick brained fucking insane bitch. Yeah, I want to scratch that fucking itch. They wait in the dark places; you don't want to meet the other faces that I've hid.

Cause you're not the first to hurt me. The dark ones are coming and they're there to usurp me, they are currently coming alive, my subconscious taking over. You best beware of my built in securities.

I wish I could make you suffer the way you do me... I wish I could take that last breathe from you, like you took my last self from me. I wish you could feel the pain of the names you been calling me. Worthless Disgrace. I know they're not my thoughts but I'm starting to believe what you spit in my face. Unable to choose a healthy escape because you took away all my choices...now I'm just full of your goddamn voices and I thought I was my own worst critic.

The best of me is dead and the worst of me is growing into the monster you awoke; it spoke to me. "Just the rest of your life in prison Katie"; sinned myself into this bad dream and I can't be woke. Hate and despair, please God help me repair my self-esteem, Cuz that would be dope... God please help me see a way out of every mistake that led me to the end of this rope.

Drawn in by an improbable wish, your promises were such luscious lips but now I can't escape the abusive abyss. Just trying to avoid your fists but your words they cut the deepest. Like open heart surgery on all my weaknesses, you tear me apart with your toxic belief system. The years of deceiving, pretending you were better than me and me always believing this. Fuck I'm just trying to find peace and shit.

So now I'm begging you to loosen your control, please let me go. Stop trying to kill what little I have left of my soul and accept me as a person who deserves to be able to grow; you

stifled my voice; you tarnished my glow. Your
denial and insults became normal... yeah you
broke me down slow.

  I was a beautiful butterfly you saw as a
nuisance reducing me to mucus to spit back in
my face when all I wanted was to be treated like
a human. But you needed someone to hate
because you can't hate yourself, you can't face
yourself; you need someone to blame for every
cell you despise of your own DNA, you can't
even drink it away, not even with that 5th a day.
Nope that whiskey won't fix thee. Neither will
the smoke or the coke but if you just beat down
on Katie you can avoid the mirror that tells the
truth, you're the weakest link, never matured
from your youth.

  So, you create this state of scrutiny and
intoxication, abuse and manipulation, my worth
according to your calculations. Underestimated
and degraded, I'm chastised and suffocated. I'm
desperate for acceptance and adoration,
something you wouldn't ever give me so
please......just stop this, Nathan.

Paramount Impairment

How do I say it, how can I utter the words? The world is so vastly complicated, and my heart is so treacherous; I do not want to fall headfirst.

I never do this right, and I never do that right, my baby can do nothing good either. Just another thing to complain about from my Step, one more imperfection boils over the seether.

My fight is silent and even when voiced there is no one to empathize with my burden. It has become such a heavy load to carry I can't see past them; I've not been able to open the curtains.

My heart is raw and stings, under confession I admit this state of disarray is nothing outside of form. I panic now as if anxiety was conceived, perhaps from my own womb, it could have been born.

The swells of emotion are violent at times, and the precipice that lies before me is plenty high for me to fall to my death. I try to breath in and out to stop the despair, as if the pain could be released through my breath.

My tears carry poison out from my soul but there is still an immeasurable amount left. In consolation I dream of a life without hearts, unless there is one out there, that is quick to proceed of thine theft.

Be still the waters within, cease the storm that churns my heart from the floor of the sea, and night. Let the pressure release slowly out, just as it was built, do not succumb to the urge to bite.

Why do I always have to be the one to rush to the battle line, why am I the one to head to the spar? If only once I was left to watch from a distance somewhat safe, somewhere put off afar.

So many fronts have to be defended I can hardly know within which one I give my brute force. But I know exactly where I shall fall if I do not get control if I let my disease take its course.

"Abandon ship! Man overboard! Run for your life! Seek Help!" All of these thoughts run through my contemplative mind. But somehow, I seem to be insubordinate to all of my ranting; I do not even give notice to the cries or yelps of the kind.

Reinforcements are necessary, put in the call! We must prepare for only the worst. The devil has bid for a tag for my toe, and is fully equipped with a headstone, a plot, and a hearse.

Whatever beauty I hold within myself is not noteworthy for this struggle of mine. If I can't get past what I fight the most all the good will have been for nothing, except a memory in time.

Relapse

Relapse, it follows me around in the dark, cold and unfeeling.

I keep waiting for it to tackle me again.

My soul aches in anticipation for it to overcome me, but my steps show no proof.

I fall into place every time wondering how it got me once again. Every tear shed is in vain.

I look both ways to make sure my path is still clear, but I stumble somehow, and when I stare at the sky as I lay on the ground, I lose feeling and the clouds seem like they move by in slow motion.

But when I get up again, I discover the world has passed me by.

Waiting In The Wings

There she goes out for a stroll; she starts her day off right. She is walking tall with her head held high; but her lips are pursed too tight.

She can only think but she cannot say, she is putting up a fight. Her mind stabs her over and over again as if it were just for spite.

She has come to a fork in the road it's hard to choose to decide which way it is to the light. So, there she stands a paradox, but will she choose left, or right?

You can only walk on one side of a fence is what she remembers from Dad. But can I choose to skip the fence when lonely, is it okay if you are sad?

The lawn is always greener from where we stand when gazing at our neighbors' grass. She wants to be happy with what she has but there is much in life she lacks.

If only there was an easier softer way, she would gladly take that direction. She has often taken the well beaten path, and stood, over and over again for correction.

She has a chance that she does not see to overcome and emerge from her past. There is much to do, a work divine, the players have all been cast.

They go about day by day, trying to learn their parts; but they must practice even harder still if they want the truth to touch their hearts.

Again and again, they execute a grand dance, a graceful but gallant show. The chorus is booming, and the performers are on beat, but when will it be her time to go?

She waits and watches, her cue has been given but she has not answered the call. What more does she need to take her turn on the stage, why on earth would she continue to stall?

She has let the world wear her down and the scar still burns and stings; She knows her family is made up of Angels......But she is still waiting in the wings.

Kassie's Song

I breathe in as I try to fight them, clouds, and I hold my breath just for a moment before it escapes into a quivering sigh. I cannot remember a time when your face was not like an angel's to me.

There is no part of space that has not captured your beauty, and yet it becomes like dust in the wind.

I watch your ship sink, because my tears could fill oceans, and my strength is but a flimsy blade of grass under a boot of a man. I can only stir my own heart and hope its warmth reaches across the sea, which keeps you in its grave.

If only my fire were hot enough to burn your capture, I would cause ashes to become of his face! But my embers cannot save even the light.

I would love to borrow some light from the stars to put in your path, but I cannot catch them. Maybe then you could find your way out of the Deep.

You have fallen, and your eyes see a candle in between the waves, so you go after it, down you go on a staircase of darkness.

Pray be the light, like on a morning when I am determined not to get out of bed. It does creep across the sill, into every corner, through the sheets, it doesn't tire.

I have only a part left of me now. I am without. Your sweet voice, can it please save me from this bitter fruit? I cannot bare the taste. I cannot bare it.

I am not as strong as the hum of waters flowing, nor am I as strong as the whisper of trees. I am not as strong as sands washed back and forth at tide, neither am I as strong as the hairs of a newborn child. I am not as strong as dried petals. I am not as strong as the voice of a man at his death, nor as strong as crumbs fallen from the loaf.

My back is turned, for I have no strength to face the shore. But I stand and weep, that my tears may influence the waves to change direction. I scream!! I beat myself!! I'd die!! But it does nothing. Please stars?! Please Moon?! Please Sun?! Hear me in desperation! And Beautiful Sailor please hear my song across your waves.... you are not forgotten.

This Is Bullshit

This is Bullshit....
While you're lying I'm trying to see past the mask you are hiding behind.
Bullshit........You wave your white flag in the air without a care that salvation from your battle is not hard to find.
Bullshit....You are so selfish; you lay claim to a self-less program just to make a name.
It's Bullshit.... How can I be inspired by the role-models who conspire only to further their own gain?
The situation at hand is you're sneaky, scandalous, and pathetic. You just don't get it. You're drawing stick figure sobriety pictures on a canvas made for Picasso; it's possible you're a Monet at best. A complete fucking mess up close, you'd best up your dose of reality before you end up comatose as a result of endorsing your fantasy. I can't believe this is the road you chose.

It's Bullshit how a pedestal can make you seem so much smarter and taller, I've never seen you smaller when it tipped over and crashed from you smoking some fucking grass. I had you up

there so long looking back, I don't think you
ever earned it or deserved it but that's my fault
for putting you up there. Without a care in the
world you sat, propped and twirled, now I'm too
dizzy, it seems you're to busy to realize people
are watching you. An audience ready to give up
applause before the act begins, just to encourage
you to share the passages. Your ignorance, faint,
and hopelessness that's how you coped with this
disease, please spare me the details of your
battles or how hard it is to overcome the rattles
or bare your load with the sport track you
decided to drive down this road with.
Son-of-a-bitch sometimes wounds don't heal,
they leave behind just enough to remind you of
the cut, never worthy enough to medicate the
pain, now what have you got to gain from giving
up?
Now I'm bleeding from your mistake, a
disadvantage. I'm finding it hard to digest this
cake a pain too unbearable to manage. Do you
hear what I'm telling you? I have been damaged
and I can't stand it.
This shit will be hard to knit into a sweater but
I'm going to make it fit turn it inside out and
wear it I swear it until I wear it out: nothing's
going to keep me warmer while my beast lay
dormant knowing it could have been me.... I
hope you make it back Stevie.

If She Only Knew

Under twenty-thousand tons of brick and stone, she carries all the weight of her own world. But somewhere deep inside, under the cartilage and bone, lies the battered heart of one little girl alone.

She is sweet like sugar, but she is bitter like the broken sugar pot. Her dad says that she can be anything she wants to be, but she only sees what she is not. With her blanket of security and the mighty force of her own will, she is treading water in her pink pajamas, she is treading water still. Hopelessly she is swimming further into the sea, thinking she is substandard, but all the while, she is beautiful to me.

She is strong and silent; she is blunt and shrewd. She thinks that nobody loves her, if she only knew.... how much that I have missed her, I always pray for you, my little sister.

Disbeliever, underachiever, don't you shed another tear. Little sister, broken heart resister, it's not like that over here.

Falling Up

In the aftermath of a drug relapse, I'm faced with the road I've chosen, where before hate melted away like ice, now again in it my fate is frozen.

The only question that remains is, whether or not this will be the time I take my last breath, on the field of my life I see the battle is lost and the war is a fight to the death.

With nowhere else to turn I turn to myself to add up the cost of my vice, with every heartbeat in my chest I consider the loss of one unlucky roll of the dice.

I look at the world stuck in the gray blind to the black and the white, on my left shoulder sits the Lord of the Darkness opposing the King on my right.

With knowledge comes responsibility not just for my life but for faces I've never even seen; no amount of money or power can serve as redemption for the continued existence of all human beings.

It does not make sense that I'm killing myself in order to feel alive, I've counted and rolled it and cashed in my change but I'm still a dollar short of a will to survive.

I'm a slave to a drug that doesn't even get me high, I would normally consider a joke, but five bucks a day is just the down payment on it, a lung for a light and a smoke.

Then there's this tower I'm trapped in, I'm waiting for my prince, I'm watching for him on his steed, but my insecurities blind me to the exit sign on the door, placed plainly for all to see.

I spend more time shopping than I used to, always on the search for the gene that fits, but the outcomes the same, insanity sewn in the seam, no matter which brand I pick.

I want to know, how was a child created, without me possessing the natural instincts of a mom? And after five and a half years we've been related, tell me why I still struggle with where he belongs.

I've been wounded so many times by back-stabbers and assassins the scars have completely covered my skin, but now as I stare at myself in the mirror, I must confess, the burns I am covered with are from my own sin.

I want to go back in time and sit on the lap of my dad, and have him whisper I'm daddy's little girl, back before I lost my innocence, back to a time I hadn't lost faith in the world.

After nine months of flying the process starts over and I find myself back in the dust again, I'll have to get out the drawing board to see where I

went wrong, what kind of morals was I supposed
to be practicing?

I don't have the strength left to wear a mask
even more less the armor of a soldier, and each
and every day I undertake the task, the weight
bears down more on my shoulders.

If my life was wrote down in a book as a
record, word for word exactly the same, I
wonder if I searched through, recalled it and
named all my sins would I be able to make sense
of the pain?

I know God can look at my life just as if he had
a copy, but he requires no pages nor ink, all I
need to do is read the part where he bought me,
if I want forgiveness of a humble
cup I must drink.

So where does this leave me, all these woes on
my mind, and I sink lower the higher I now get,
I fail to realize the satisfaction in life I might
find if I could only let go of my fix.

Ballad Of Deceit

I woke up feeling crazy today, likely to be lost in my haze today, and the burn of my insecurities they're so pure to me I can't see past it. But on the other side of this hit, I see clearly, and I do not fear nearly as much.

No crutch day to day as I pass up temptation, the storm takes away from me throughout the duration leaving me weak. But I long for the other side of this Vic it's like it makes me strong more likely to hold on.

Then I have all these thoughts racing through my head, manic episodes where I'd rather be dead, my confusion is fed by a hundred emotions hitting me all at the same time. In my mind, I feel relief at this point, is on the other side of a joint.

Maybe then I could let my hair down, let loose. So far, I've been forced to choose too many hours at work all this responsibility hurts, no one sees what I have to go through to relax a little. But on the other side of this needle there's a calm so real as the raw courses through my arm, and no one can harm me, and I can be charming.

Normally I can't seem to socialize with my peers without tears of frustration I want to be heard but I'm incapable, defective, there's no salvation from the burn. I'm dying to feel free. You know, on the other side of this Ecstasy I never had a problem collecting friends for the weekend, there was a ton of them, and we always had fun together.

Now the ties have been severed and I'm stuck worrying too much about life and the people in my world, it's like a truck has been hurled at my face and the voices are hard to escape, I can't get away! I might need a shrink or maybe some time to go think. But on the other side of this drink everything is lost in translation, and I feel found at whatever the cost.

I'm tired of fostering feelings of being left out and separate, I'm tired of feeling desperate. I'm so filled with anger it dances in my eyes, what a surprise I can control what I feel. But on the other side of this pill, I could care less who I kill, and I don't have to feel anything for you, no mercy for the pitiful.

I think it's strange that I try as hard as I do to change and all you want is more, tell me what exactly is the wage I get paid to perform? I'm not an act, but my whole life is a lie. But on the other side of this high honesty is all I see, and there's no stage. There's just me.

I'm faced constantly by inadequacies and when I don't feel pretty, and my mind does not believe

that I look just fine. On the other side of this
line, I'm reminded of my beauty and there is
nothing your jealousy can do to me.

I hate that I can be so vulnerable, and I don't
want to depend on you to get me through, but
now it's hard to undo what I've found to be true.
On the other side of this dope, it gets easier to
cope and whether or not it's real doesn't matter
because I've already forgotten why I've
slammed back a shot, and before it even reaches
my throat I feel better.

Whether its hate from exposure, pain with no
closure, love that's not real, or I'm anxious to
feel, unfaithful friends with no one to depend on,
fear turned to rage, my mind as a cage, losing
my soul with only pride to fill the hole, I've got
to remember. On the other side of this cry there's
a chance I'll get by, if I never forget why I put
down the High.

In The Mud

Her hair is pale and golden blond; it's thin and whispers delight. Her dress is navy blue with a collar; her shoes are gleaming white.

Her hair is combed and lies straight down; the dress has been neatly pressed.
Her shoes are new and somewhat stiff; she is five or six, if guessed.

She is waiting to go out to play; she taps her foot to a beat not heard.
She stands and shuffles her shoes on the ground; she whistles the tune of the birds.

She peers out the window to look at the world; the grass looks lush and green. There are flowers in the field that she wants to pick; she puts her nose to the glass and screen.

Her shoes are white, and the dirt is brown, the predicament is unknown to her. She thinks it is hard to turn the large brass handle; she strains as if it were.

Light and wind touch her face; the sun is warm to the skin.
She stands with all her grace and wonder; where on earth will she begin?

Her dress is clean, and her socks are white with ruffles; her shoes still possess their shine. The

afternoon holds uncertainties for her; her shoe
tips touch the porch, and pine.

Her gaze is set upon a creek; cat tails line the
water course.

Her dress grazes her legs as it's blown in the
wind, she has no fear or remorse.

Her steps are light but purposeful; she walks
across the yard.

Her socks have dew upon them now, she holds
no wisdom, and she knows no scars.

She is almost there; she thinks this is where she
was meant to go.

Her confidence is unwavering, how much more
could she need to know?

She reaches out to grab the stems, her foot
hovers over the ground.

Her last step forward towards the creek has
turned her white shoe brown.

Her eyes see the clouds above; she has slipped
into the muddy muck. Her thoughts are
confused; she tries to, but she is unable to get
up.

Her dress is saturated and soiled; she tries to
detain her cries. She pushes the hair back from
her face; the mud gets in her eyes.

She stifles her tears now; her composure is
built within.

She must rise up from the ground; her will turns
up her chin.

She grabs a hold of her senses; she has faith
inside her heart.
She stands and sees her reflection in the water,
she is reluctant to depart.

Her dress is spoiled, and her shoes are scraped,
she hopes her mother will understand. She walks
back towards her home; she holds no flower in
her hand.
Her stride is lacking, her spirit is ashamed. Her
door is heavier than normal, her ignorance she
blames.

She meets her mother in the hall; the dress is
caked in mud.
She follows the cracks in the floor with her gaze,
her knees fold to the floor with a thud.

Her mother picks her up and takes her down
the hall; the giant tub is filled with warm water.
She cannot feel the cold anymore, the mother
shampoos her daughter.

Her dress is thrown into the trash; she is given
a clean new frock. Her new dress beams of
white, her hair returns to golden locks.

She knows now of the mud that holds captive,
her flower remains the cost. Her new dress will
not be tainted, but her innocence forever lost.

Look Back

She's looking back upon the past; she's looking back and running fast. She sees the bad and hates the pain; she loves the thought of never again.

She moves forward and sees no one behind, she never looks back to see their crying. She hates the guilt, it's like she never felt it, she makes herself forget, but she cannot help it.

She doesn't think of her life before, as anything but a huge, closed door. She won't go back to see; what it is she gave up to be.

She thinks she is safe and secure in his arms, and she thinks that her life is pure, she fears no harm.

She thinks that she has everyone she needs, but far behind her, her family bleeds.

She is beautiful, but burned, and there are lessons she has learned. She holds her head up high and forgets them with a sigh.

What horrors lay behind her is what her close friends remind her. But does she see the mirror on the wall, if she only looked in it, her defenses might fall.

Can she love and forgive, even though her heart plays dead. She loves to recall the pain, but how much can she stand to gain.

She tells herself they are a family new and better, but neglects to see, that they have just met her. There is a place behind, far, far away that holds hands, bends knees, and prays.

That place is wet with tears and echoes of scars, some of them are from her, and some of them are theirs.

Those left behind cannot forget the roads they have paved, but she goes forward without thinking of the ones she made.

She is so misunderstood from all that was before, but in the future, she sees love and hope restored. There it is, all around, the world is where she now feels found.

There is no hope for those behind, they cover their eyes, they just cry and cry. They have no choice but to watch and see, their poor lost child fall desperately.

She holds her baby close to her as she wishes, she could say goodnight, instead of goodbye kisses.

If only she had stopped her hate, if she had only forgiven, but now it's too late.

Sober

Cigarettes in my pocket, gas in my tank, things trivial in life but they make me feel the safe-ness, like a warm kiss they keep me holding onto this idea of security has got me twisted.

If the expulsion of hope doesn't show on my face, then it's bound to show the expulsion of my faith. Sober coping, unforeseen this bad dream, never telling never selling the ending.

How comical the battle with the Devil for my soul is (like bloody noses), my spiritual growth is the answer to my questions. I can't rest in this place.

The carbon copy of this attention whore's life is proof I can't let go of my greedy plight. I want something you can't give, a new me. But I kid myself into the possibility.

Change should be like paint-by- numbers do the work for me, so I can take advantage of the sweet slumber that comes with normality.

Trying to make sense of this road of abstinence, this conscience as consequence of entering repentance.

Can I ever see past my own eyes of vanity if I never turn inside to see the sanity-in. That's backwards placed wrong in hindsight, the

mirrors of my mind lie. Snow White, Snow
White you must die.

Forgive and forget promise freedom from
resentment, but what when the bitch that kills
you takes up residence in your tent? Your
temple? Ha! My body hasn't been that well
respected in my fantasies, no use of planning of
redemption.

I'm kept in suspense, when I try to see the road
less traveled, I commence, on a journey the path
turns me away from self-will, the riot that so
quietly killed me.

My confusion is greatly amplified when I try to
fight the urge to purge the affliction on the
inside. I'm discouraged. But I can flourish, with
only 12 steps-13 is too many. But can He that is
Holy relieve the pain and console me into
righteousness, so he has not to destroy me?

Good God, I have a helper, cause to become a
shelter of love straight down from above so my
spirit my soar as the doves. Because I've been
fighting traffic the wrong way all this time,
when push came to shove, I was bound to get
mine, but time is running out.

Katie put down, put down, put down the... oh
my God I'm feeling sick. The answers to my
problems are beginning to stick inside my head;
I'm fed the nutritious meal of knowledge.

So, what else can I call it? Hi, my name is
Katie and I finally figured that I'm an alcoholic.
I frolic in the acceptance of my addiction. My
conniption at the fiction of graduation is the
realization that, that degree of salvation is for a
dead man.